No Man's Land

"A collection of observatory poems"

Ajit Yadav (Aky)

Made with ❤ on the BookLeaf Publishing Platform
www.bookleafpub.in
www.bookleafpub.com

Dedication

I have been very gracious of all the people who have been a part of my life and have helped me to do better in my endeavours and I shall always be grateful for that.

I want to dedicate this book to my mother who has unintentionally infused in me the inquisitiveness of exploring with literature with her story telling skills and her oscar winning acting performances. I cannot even imagine penning a single word without her support and push towards my decisions in life. But, I can only lament the fact that she isn't here to read this or hear the poems I have written.

My gratitude to my friends, my brothers and my loved ones who with their anger, love and care have always tried to make me a better person. I hope and pray that this collection meets your reading taste.

Regards,
Ajit Yadav

Preface

*These poems are reflective of my work, my observations
and some personal odes that have taught me about life
and its way around. Some poems are written to evoke a
sense of idea on the message that I have learned through
my own experience of life.*

*It revolves around the notions of love, human nature,
some are downright dystopian and some utopian but
with a gist of my observations and my intellect. I have
strived to present a picture of the world that I have
explored in each poem. The themes are a mixed of
human errors, struggles of living in a human society and
a pinch of political, social upheavals which I have
witnessed is reflected in the poems.*

*Of all the poems, "Living without Mom," is an ode to my
ma and here I try to exonerate my emotional attachment
which could connect to any person who has gone though
a human lost.*

*Some are stories that couldn't be penned down in prose
but with poetry and I have tried to take as much freedom
as possible in trying to paint the sketch of the story or*

the idea that struck me to write.

I write with certain emotions and images that I have seen through being in any situation and it is that ability to feel something with so much of depth that has pushed me to go ahead and describe it in the format that is suitable for describing it.

In conclusion, I can only say that it is the joy of vision that enables me to create a world which is purely to lash out what's felt in my subconscious but it is more importantly a task which comes with heavy load when it is to be read by others and expected to be read in their own interpretations. I only hope and pray that it is read with the same values and emotions that I have tried to sprinkle through the words of "No Man's Land."

Acknowledgements

I would like to express my deepest gratitude to my teachers through out my journey from school to college. It is your patience that has made me comprehend some of the most complex portions of literature to also push the envelope in making a nasty boy like me to go hard on reading and to acquire as much knowledge as I can to built on it and create something of my own.

Sir Tripathi, thank you for mentoring me during my higher secondary days and listening to my problems and providing the best solutions possible and most importantly, this book would still be a dream if you had not made an impression on me with your powerful vocabulary and great story telling skills. I shall always be in debt to the knowledge you have imparted on me.

Sir Achuth, you are one such brilliant mind that I have met in my life who have always made me think and rationalise with myself and the choices I made with my life. You truly are one intellectual that makes one feel intellectual in return too. Well, at least I felt that. Please don't tell me I am wrong. I am very humbled by your constant teachings and I hope I have made a good attempt in using the knowledge that you have inculcated in me.

Sir Selvin, Lenore, evermore.
I hope that rings some bells to your consciousness. Thank you for being my mentor during the dissertation phase of my college. I am very excited to receive your feedback on the work that I have done. I hope I have managed to withhold your expectations to the optimum. Thank you for being the soul that you are and to ignite me with aspirations by being such an inspiration.

Mam Vinci, Mam Amen, Mam Betina, Sir Ajith, Mam Sunanda, Sir Rajesh, Sir Limathung, I also want to give my gratitude to you with folded hands in hope that my quirky behaviour is excused and forgiven and in return, I get your blessings for the upcoming endeavours.

My father has been a guide and the source that makes me wanna work all day and night and have no regrets whatsoever. Thank you baba for being who you are and providing me the learning of life in your own capacity.

My brothers have many a times bore the brunt of my deeds and I am apologetic and thankful for their support and unconditional love. You make my life easy by taking some of the difficulties off my shoulder.

And special thanks to Mishika, my dear student and more of a little sister for igniting the motivation to just go on with the writing and that's how "Seeds," came about.

1. Reflections

Someday we will talk
Like the days we had a word as we walk
at the footpath dreaming the future's path
like the flowers of the spring that face the autumn's wrath.
Someday we shall meet
like the days we intimidated like a tweet
at the jokes and laughter we shared
near the expectations' room that we feared.
Someday we shall dance
like the ducks jamming to rainwater like addicted to trance
at the music of complete love
that doesn't miss a beat like the composition of a serene dove.
Someday we shall truly be human
regardless of all follies and be no showman
at the repeated hymns of passersby
that makes our appearance deceitful for the claim of lovers-by.
Some day we shall be together
like the root to the white rose forever
at the dawn of the funeral of the evil spirit that lights

when we burst the bubble of judgement and see our
hearts that lights.

2. Geometry

Shadows appear because men live,
what doesn't make sense is the attribute to give

One works and jerks in life,
but not knows for whom is all the strife,

It still goes on like governments,
regardless of any real increments.

Ever wondered, why the pain and agony?
Ever wondered, why in spite of the blood, it is a made up
symphony?

It is the burden of family
or the societal hilly-billy?

Never can one find the answer that rhymes
with the notions of world-class wisdom that chimes.

It is a question's question
that takes life's cushion.

Still the nail and soil like the rails weighted by trains

It never stops to reason why but to toil instead in rains.

The cycle tires that spins has spikes
like the nature's beauty has rocks that makes one yikes!

It is the shadow that men live for
But not live for the light that is birth's core.

What's left then is a geometry
that one tries to live up to till cemetery.

Cemetery of every geography
in god's choreography.

3. Seeds

Seeds that are burrowed beneath
Shall see the growth indeed
But life's a snail
that needs to sail
And seeds like snails needs a nail
for reaching the fourth corner of the soil
And nail's a pesticide
to multiply and to set aside
that brings indeed the life out
and provides life for a shout
As you- Mishika, the seed- that is grown
like the seed that works for pain- you shall too one day
be known.
To mankind and naysayers
who will claim to be your ancestors.

4. Death to live

It was a party that was lively
all went in eagerly

But all but two were seen but not seen
in the midst of the weary scene.

One was a loner
the other was perhaps loner- to be sooner

They giggled and figgled
but not jiggled and wiggled

All they did was to impersonate
and mimic they made look passionate

Lines and lines went by for the two
of public and friends who knew what the two went into

But the crowd knew nothing
that went into insides of both growing

They smile, laugh, clap and rap
but wail, cough, tap and gap

of each other's mortal ranges
that went into the fictional ganges

But they are lively and eager
like the juvenile tiger

Someone took them away
to rot and sway

In memories of blood
that killed both in its flood

One sided and tried
other misguided and pried

Alas, they looked at each other's eyes
wanting to clasp like dyes

But they know not who they are
for they are ashes joined in atoms rare

rare that stares
as their soul flares.

Soul prys and yearns
that they couldn't earn.

Shoulder -to- shoulder that couldn't become
now are standing as imposters to welcome.

The elf that perhaps has had one of them
that is no longer soul but mechanics packaged like a
gem.

That shines but is nothing
but mirage in shining

letting the party go on
I see the two live on

But in vain
as it rains.

5. What's black is a rack

What's black is a rack
of words and actions filled in a sack

That drips of droplets of blood that's hot
of colour that wraps the ashes' pot

still black is a wack
of indignities and obscenity that shows crack

wide enough that shows all flimsy
that men and women do in all whimsy

to prove a worth that's not worth to existence
but still dare to live in subsistence

what's blacker than black?
that allows to cut a slack?

It is the dream of other colours
that makes the black do rounds of hell's parlour

so, black is as real as real
that dreams to assimilate into the colours of reel.

that's packed and rolled and bowled from wall to wall
Hoping and gaping and squeaking from box to box that
stands tall and tall

with a little hole in it to see a vision
that has colours that turns into a mission

and that's what is oblique
that looks like a plaque

because what's black is a rack
of words and actions filled in a sack

and one day, a truck comes
and the sack dumps.

6. Hammer and Nail

There goes my eyes shut dreaming
of the clock that ticked all with weeping
no tears but sweat dripping
that salty mushy fluid slipping
my heart pumps two beats a second to work round
knowing that it is to come again to soak sound
ground is the abode to Allah
ash is the atom to Krishna Kanhaiya
are also the names that comes to tongue in dusty coal
but the stripes of the lords are no mercy to it to roll.
the hoe and spade have seen the crime in mine
that can't speak but can pardon by breaking into pieces
to give time.
For rest and food
not to test for good.
There goes my eyes into dreaming
of dreams and dreams full of cream
no stale bread and poison h2o
that reminds me of embryo
only taste that is for rest a waste
but to us a delicacy that is to chase
for clothes fancy
to be named hancy

then goes my eyes open with a song
to the sound of the diabolical gong.
I get up and shit in a pit
then see food like a sin
the spade and hoe become Thor's hammer
that only I understand without a stammer.
The smell of swine comes from the mine
then I walk like Moses but see dark in shine,
as I go deeper, I see a nail dripping red
I stopped there to see if there is a bed
to wake me from dreaming
of the clock that's ticking but now I am weeping
as the visual of me hanging in nails terrifies
as my soul crucifies.

7. No Man's Land

I stood on the no man's land,
Land, where truth prevails in every handful of sand,
Was it ok for me to dilapidate the convivial relationship
of sentient beings with nature?
I frained,
To stand defiant against all obstructions of dissent to
establish my stature,
I frained.

Nada did I perceive out of the sinister, I made it feasible,
Nada did I achieve out the Ministers, I made it
conceivable,

But why am I talking about it now and who am I talking
to?
Is my breath still blowing in the wind or is it just the fear
of annihilation which I foresee from my palace of doom?
Why talk about it now when the absurd time was busy
negotiating about the apocalyptic impact of the
detonation?
I think I know why.
Because nothing's left on the man's land I became a big
brother of.
****

With my steady steps in the radioactive no man's land, I
forged my way
Yearning for the touch of the droplets of dawn.
But, my hands were incompetent to do so for everything
is contaminated in no man's land.
The colorless tears rolled down as I grudgingly moved
forward
Yearning for the touch of the droplets of dawn.
In doing so, I walked past a tree, I would sit under the
shade of;
I continued walking and frowned at the plastic foot
marks, leaving me
Yearn for the old long rejuvenated breathe of nature,
which is now,
An intangible potion.
I wanted to stand naked and inhale the air of the tree,
but in vain for it is
An intangible potion.
****

Am I free of radiation by wearing plastic?
If yes, then for how long?
I've turned the myth of king Midas into reality.
Everything I desire to touch is untouchable.
Who am I? Am I God?
Is being God devoid of sense and judgement?
Was the testament right or did I make it right?
Who is to be blamed, the creator of God, God itself or the

follower of the creator of God who believed in God?
***

As I walked, I had a rumination:
I planned for nuclear
But had no notion that, it would escalate nu-clear
By nu-clearing everything on the land
 I intended to be sinister for.

Combustion happened, sentient beings melted,
And I had my homecoming about the catastrophe,

Alas, Sapiens defiled,
Making nucleus to refile .

Whom shall I exercise my regime on?
Whom shall I be a big brother for?

For no man's land has stretched its boundaries with
apparent no man,
Only radiation. Omniscient radiation.
Heil Hitler! Rossiya veperyod! Jai Shree Ram!
******

I am walking on the no man's land
Where truth prevails in every handful of sand singing
my favorite song:
যদি তোর ডাক শুনে কেউ না আসে তবে একলা চলো রে
"If nobody listens to you, walk alone."

8. Mark Antony's World

We live in Mark Antony's world
and rejoice the chair's lord

He came to bury Ceasar
we bury ourselves in cold freezers

He gathered the crowd to prove
we rather are proud to groove

to the tales of their tactics
we do the sales of their politics

For Mark Antony made all murderers honourable
we make dark symphony of all intruders conquerable.

He talked about Ceasar's refusal to kingship thrice
we walked about Lord's appraisal to chair-ship thrice

To bumble and rumble
to wrestle and gamble.

We live in Mark Antony's world at word
But give in to jerk symphony Lord at cord

No battles to cry for and to jump
as no beetles to pry for and to get dump

at Mark Antony's world we find peace
to only speak and to ponder when minced.

9. Blades of Scissors

Abstract patterns of kaleidoscope
Is tangible to the eyes like mirrors.
Only difference is the lack of hope, which blurs the
Time-Travel face like clinging blades of Scissors.

At first, I saw the cheeks filled with pink marbles and felt
dirty as against the person, wondered, how can
a man be so ugly and yet have the audacity,
To walk in the midst of multitudes?

Fast forward and the person was me, looking nervous
and walking with notions of prying eyes
scrutinizing me from head to toe, making me realize the
ferocity.
And the myth of ugliness altered with a novel attitude.

Abstract patterns of kaleidoscope
Is tangible to the eyes like mirrors,
Only difference is the experience of hope, Which is more
blurry to my Time-Travel sub – conscious,
Making me clinch my incisors.

At second, I saw the hooligan, screaming at his lungs

Dressed like a Buffon with moronic intelligence.
A time lapse occurred and the Buffon was me - jigging
for nationalism only to get into the realm of
sympathizing reality where you get converted into
hunks.
The pattern becomes visible to you at this stage by the
stature of your presence.

At third, I saw the failing scholar with words of
grandiloquent barking with a spirit of possessing elixir-
like brilliance.
The pattern becomes a little translucent and the
confidence of endowing thyself with proper direction is
given to the scholar with the omniscient allegiance.

And the process begins
To re-invent a Messiah for the world to radicalize the
status quo.

Pages by pages, orations after orations, sexuality to
sexuality, Myth to myth , barter to money, money to
economy, farming to Farmers, labor to laborer, big filthy
asses to big filthy stomachs, of men to women,
of women to trans genders, eunuchs to gays, lesbians to
bisexuals.

And that's not enough ..

Perhaps, it is never enough.

From fire to language, from language to agriculture,
agriculture to civilization, from civilization to
dehumanization.

Things will change
Things have changed
Things are changing
Things keep changing
The word 'Thing' has changed too...

But where is the pattern to define kaleidoscope?
I can't find the co- ordinates to be precise.
Is it the present or the presence
Is it the past or the pasts

Am I moving or moved
Am I humming or hummed
Am I travelling or travelled
Am I living or have I lived?

A thin flash of current is observed before my
hallucination is over and in it,
A pattern is seen, a pattern of a pattern,
Undecipherable.

I am awake now, may be now is not now and now is
never now

But where am I going with the awakening?
To awaken the awakened who choose to slumber over
the D- Day?
Or

Am I just in a limbo?

Will figure out, for now,
I shall sleep.
As I slept,

Abstract patterns of kaleidoscope
Is tangible to the eyes like mirrors.
Only difference is the lack of hope
Which blurs the Time-Travel face
Like clinging the blades of scissors.

10. The last knock on the door of the light

Oh beloved man,
who gave thee a reasonable life,
do know that a man without a clan
lives all his life in a strife

count the days to live,
you say, for your blazing arrogance
has extinguished, leaving you to dive
into the pit of filthy fragrance.

sniff the dirt you man,
and the vulnerable homecoming
of your lethargy to your woman
for having a black heart melting

for the melting stinks
and pushes me to the brim to kill
your shenanigans while Yamraj brings
overwhelming joy to fill.

but, I am gun free
with an anti-spirit for all being

for all the Asur in me is in spree
to devour your hope of spring

but no beloved
man, I would be jovial with you,
kind with you, in fact, I have behaved
and sold my soul to be you.

and your struggle to
the last knock on the door of the light
will be walked and carried against-to
the pyre vanquishing plight

of a dynasty,
and the living phoenix resurrects
to turn my impotent-fantasy
real and end the genesis.

11. Uphill

There is a black shadow that clouds
over the mountains that looks like a shroud

the trees are serene and florescent
like the innocence of adolescence

These are images I see as I climb up the hill
to ponder about my last will

to be credited to my children all for free
to enjoy the labour and savour the fruits of the tree

I made and grew from a seed
hoping it never turns into a weed.

But that's a reverie as a father
because I know it will turn into ashes from the big
brother

as they are made of soft skin and cream
they have no idea of the many screams

I had to endeavour

to give them the demeanour

of no righteousness and brightness
of thought and wellness

but instead of pride and no strive
to work and rework and thrive.

And I walk through the mountains
seeing the wails of animals in terrains

they see me with frantic eyes and then when I look at
their lenses
they see the pain and agony and change their view and
their senses

I use a stick and walk with pace
finding the pace to race

with life in solitary confinement
to seek life in refinement.

Up the hill I go
Reading my will I go

then comes a step covered with snow and no surface
and I step on it and let go of the life without a preface

down the hill I see spectators with tears
and I pass my tears like pears

and at the speed of the light, I fall with a thud and fluid
splashed
and my skull broke open and I saw my son weeding
completely mashed.

And down the hill I went with my will
and everything went against my will.

12. Bill

Here comes the uphill
that resounds of the snow hills

that makes one to come more
only to make one feel allure

the view is one that makes you not blink once
the lights shimmer like it has never been and makes one
to think twice

But a top the hill stands a man with a bill
still, to wish the bill as a will

that changes everything to gold
and makes one very bold

to stand in crowd
with the hair in the chest proud

and growl with every person that prowls
and then can the man brawl

over the mightiest creature on earth

and can then perhaps not repent on his birth.

here comes the wind moving the hair
making the man dream of the chair

that changes the decision
with precision

for flying with the wind
disappearing in the atom of his mind.

Now, comes the phoenix
and the man screams through his larynx

the bill burns
and its ashes runs

but the onlookers stood still with no pacifier
as the bird takes the man in arms and burns and fuses
and becomes Lucifer.

Then all came in flame
the man took the blame

and the hill
later became just another bill.

13. The fallacy of the heart

The fallacy of heart
There is a poem to recite, can I recite?
Forget it, I don't think you want to hear it.
That too from a Sapien like me.
Still, my heart doesn't agree, if not for you all,
For my conscience, I shall recite.

This body is forty years old now,
Enough things have been seen by these eyes,
Enough things have been heard by these ears,
Enough things have been said by these lips,

However, the lotus flower that blooms
From this heart and accomplices to
Oust and forget all that has been seen, heard and said, is now,
Decaying, dying, beg your pardon, perhaps is dead.

Decaying, dying, dead
How synonymous do they sound!

Seems like a talk we had about yesterday
Like it is the talk of the heart

Neither do we repent, nor do we question.
It binds the heart
As if the brain is not a part of this body.

Now, the brain reminds me,
Did you bring yours?
Your brains?
Because I forgot to bring it.

As far as I can remember
The moment I turned fourteen
My maa and baba had demanded to keep the brain in the
freezer.
Then what,
Since then, it is lying there.
I never felt the need of it
Because heart makes everything feasible, everyone said
that, even you people had said it.
Therefore, listen to this poem
With your heart.

To narrate the story of the heart,
Time is absorbed.

Now, the time reminds me
That yes, a sparkling object was hovering in the sky,
I felt strange but couldn't imagine myself to that height

because my heart didn't agree listening to other hearts.
In the midst of the chit chat, I forgot to recite the poem.
The thing is, I'm thinking with my heart,
If I had used my brain, then perhaps, I would have erased
the mistakes of the fourteen years old me.

Anyway, I am or I am not, you tell me
Because this body's worth is dissipating,
Not through my brain, but with my heart.
Because, high altitudes are not to be reached, sparkling
objects are not to be touched.
Only, listen to your heart, heart is everything,
Therefore, perceive the poem from your own heart,
Without a word, rhyme, tone and rhythm.
Because, only a murderer can hide a mystery from itself
That mystery, which comes from the brain, not the heart.

14. Living Without Mom

What's living without a mom?
ever thought of it with rum?

let me think for you
and then you can see for me too

but first cheers to life
that gives a stab with a knife.

without mom, there shall be no one
to learn how to comb

there shall be none to slap after a fall
when you weep after you burn your hand with a bomb
tall

without her, there can be no definition of love and anger
together
to keep on from becoming a monster and a human
forever.

With her, there is always a treatment to sickness

without her, there is no medicine to a disruption to
wellness.

Her hands work like a genie
that can change all dramas of me, a weenie.

A single touch of her puts you in sleep
and a single tear of her puts your soul to weep deep.

My mother, dances to make us laugh
and brings the hospital of medicines when we cough.

Her care knows no bounds
but none to see her wounds round.

She cooks, brooms, cleans and scolds,
puts the clothes, sleeps and folds

advises father to be a father
rather than a chapter

of failures and trials to us
so we don't miss the bus.

She has desires too but she puts her tongue out and cuts
all dreams
only to give those to us so we can have a life full of

cream.

She is a storyteller, an Oscar winner
and a vengeful theatrical artist to tv serial sinner.

At times, she is off to bed
all waiting for her to get set

and begin the work she dies with two hands
or as she describes with ten-head-ten hands.

Living without mom is where peace is omniscient
living without mom is where peace is actually never
present.

But I am drunk,
like the school boy that bunks

from all responsibilities of school
that could make possibilities of soft life like a wool.

But like the ignorance of school-boy
we guarded the arrogance of joy

of the weight that my mother bore
without making any roar.

The only wish she ever had
was for me to not be a brat

and to build a shanty house
that could keep in a mighty mouse

that could be ours to call
that none can force to fall.

My mama was a fighter, a singer, an iPhone user
that swore at times only because the other was an
abuser.

Soon came time that didn't rhyme
with the testament of time.

Her head got down
and it always frowned

of all pain and wail
being her support and tail

to toilet and bathing,
to eat and caressing

to needless and madness
to intensive care wellness.

Its a journey in motion where days becomes hours and
hours becomes seconds
only to see the panic and tension that stays for present
day pretentious weekends.

From the school rank
to blood bank.

I saw my mother rest
and she was in no test.

Her pyre burned
my eyes churned.

All vanquished
and languished and quished.....

Let me breathe a little!

But I found my mom,
and not when I was having a rum

but in the house she walked,
in the memories she talked,

in the utensils she washed,

in the smell of her clothes thrashed

in the chores of the house
or the smell of the dish.

My mother is in the mirror inside me
guiding or blinding me to scissor the outside of me.

That's living without a mom
with a rum

and I drink
and wink

at my mom in sunrise
and she kisses me from paradise.

15. Killed as One Soul

To all the racists monks,
Do introspect your conscience
for it has vanquished.

Vanquished in a war
where the heroes and the villains
are killed as one soul

where the soul is soul-less
as the dirt it carries is heinous
with no smell of innocence.

It alters on purpose
which gives blood coins to devour
to ugly angels of hypocrisy

who use the race as a potion,
to ensure love lorn

of sentient beings
for it has been the basis
for wiping the earth

of which we have been
the face representative
who always fail to

understand this notion
for it is the plight we indoctrinated.

16. Shakespeare's world

In Shakespeare's world we have a lot to cover
to uncover

let me explain
to suspend

all your reservations
about its preservation.

Macbeth is a phase of the world where the lover is the
precious possession
that one wants to grab with aggression.

Then, comes Hamlet where the mother surrounds the
breath and bread
and is the sole tread

to all aims and whims of epiphany
of man and his tyranny.

Then comes Othello, where the pretentious believe of
words that stands as postulates
making one to wonder about the mirror's reflection and

speculate

leading to bloodshed
underneath a tree shed or any shed.

Then comes the Merchant of Venice,
that can convince

any human to be a fool
and to never learn from school

and make arguments with no rationale
and then pretend to be the Samaritan that consumes no
ale.

Then, comes his imagery of true minds
and fills ours heart with unconditional love than one
can't find

an yet the clouded picture remains poignant
and not like the pungent lust that is stagnant.

Hence, Shakespeare's world revolves with all the stages
described
but prescribed

through the lenses of each stories

of downfalls and glories

that is described in nutshell in rage
in "All the world's a Stage."

and that's the Shakespeare's world we swirl
and after a while, underneath it, we crawl.

17. Hole

The world is a pole
and up there stands a pole
and there stands the man with an axe
beholding the fate of arrogance that was flexed
because my dual personality
has out shown my reality.
Here I am in a darkness
praying with salty sweat climbing in hope of whiteness
but the rope is thorny
making me feel how life is crony
free of all realities
and entities
only a mirage
of bricks and mortars snuggling in a garage
which needs repair
for life to pair.
Then u go up with one palm to another
with pants slipping and falling to pack of panthers
howling and waiting for a chance
to make my body dance
with flesh and quench
of bones and to smash my body like tractors over plants
at a ranch.

I am climbing with one grab after other
not knowing how to tell the big brother
to forgive and let me pass my soul
and to carry my blood in a bowl.
Alas! I reached up there
and it is here where the elf saw my gold hand and stared.
Then, he grabbed me by shoulder
and took my naked watered body out of the boulder.
He raised his axe to slice
I took my gold hand and raised as a price
The axe changed to gold
and I ran bold.
The man held the gold and dark clouds covered him
he then was thrown down the hole that spewed molten
lava on him
and that's how I got out of the hole
by giving up the gold that brought my soul
and now the winds soak my sweat
and I can live my life neat
where the peace is in the garden of Eden resides
where in God awaits in his court where he presides.

18. Crown

When the people around you
stop surrounding you

and the world is an apocalypse for you,
keep your head high and believe in you.

If everything looks blurry
and you keep feeling hungry

continue your lust until you pass
the finish line covered with lime on the grass.

What bothers you? The traffic, the taunts, the laughter
What you have to counter? The craft. The silence and the
action that sounds louder.

Then, go ahead, keep your head high
when questioned, just breathe and sigh.

They will tell you everything is wrong with you, and
nothing's practical
but you go ahead, not willing to stab, slap or clap in

drama, just be cynical

only then, there will be a miracle
of dreams that will become an oracle.

Eat less, think more, drink less, read more,
be no careless, be galore, be no selfless, be a human
evermore.

But when all that works out, do keep everything wrong
in the world out
and try bringing in novel ideas with all stout.

Don't blow your own trumpet,
neither keep any puppet,

Just try to be in your axis and maintain the singularity
making sure to maintain the arc on your gravity with
less popularity

Only then, will you become the king that gives
and not one that takes,

and only then, you shall get the invisible crown
from the grey world that that's actually brown

in its habits and then you shall learn a secret imparted

which you should keep from your mind deleted

that is of a one-eyed blindness of a real habit
just like a rabbit

that sees every thing
but pretends its nothing

and that's what you will change
in a big range.

19. To Love in Vacuum

As I sat in the lockdown days,
I had a reverie and in that:
I saw an enchanting beauty one lucky day,
Like Stars in the night sky.
She wore skinny pants and an unnamed dress
It hit my retina with love like the humid of the iron
press.
I saw an enchanting beauty one lucky day,
Like Stars in the night sky.
I entered a room and saw her muttering and pattering
I felt timid and bothered about her presence,
But we ended up with , "Whatever"
"Whatever" later became uttering what-ever to each
other.
With time, I was told she is fond of me,
But, I disbelieved cause I saw the love she had for her
love
And the love they had for each other.
I saw an enchanting beauty one lucky day
Like Stars in the night sky.
There was this night we met unexpectedly
I sought a fight with her love unexpectedly. I passed
through her pretentiously

Didn't gesticulate intentionally,
She was before my eyes,
With her black dress, the sky was clear,
I held her hand, brought her closer to my lips,
Sensed her breathe with mine,
Saw her fear of betrayal for her love, in her eyes.
Then,
My dream got shattered, I came to reality.
She was standing there, with her ability
Waiting for her love with stability.
The moon lost it's vision,
And I was left with only one precision
To rewind the next day into:
"The night we met"
Four years later,
Miles and Miles away, we separated,
The moon was kind enough, enough to make us believe that
We were close to each other despite being miles and miles away.
The stars combined and formed a shape,
Perhaps, longing to show that we are not far,
And indeed very close,
The stars make us realize how close we are to each other.
I could see the same star she could see from her distance,
What I heard as a rumour altered it into a fact, But her fact towards her love remained the same and strongest.

I do not know how I fell in love with her enchanting
beauty,
But, I do know it will not be easy to be her love for her
Love is still in her sub- conscious...
"Memories live with us to create more memories"
But I only wish not to see myself as her memory while
she dwells
With her sub-conscious love.
And if I ever became her memory and a past like she
describes
Her love as a measure of past and present,
I would only say,
I saw an enchanting beauty one lucky day,
Like Stars in the night sky.
And she became my Jasmine,
And I became her Aladdin,
And both lived happily for sometime.
Then I woke up sitting in my armchair.
And I had received a message from her.

20. The Bright Lights

When the four walls you see
the more in a square less than to be,

retaining your imagination alive,
restoring your patience to not let your frustration
overcome.

Is what you do with the four walls you see
the more in a square less than to be

when night makes you nocturnal sleeplessly;
and when day comes, you have no clue of the time that's
asking you,

What will you do with my seconds, minutes, and hours?
the only thing you can do

is to gaze the roof top, gaze the door, gaze the bed, gaze
everything surrounding you,
but your ability to sought what you are doing
worthwhile is what is called insomnia.

You become a prisoner for an uncommitted crime;

people asking you to reason for your crime,

but you have no answer to verbally speak at all;

is what you do with the four walls you see
the more in a square less than to be.

But that's not enough,
Sometimes, you peep out of the room and see the road,

And,
when you look up the road to define you,

you get into a dilemmatic momentum, to refine you,
Stones, rollers, chemicals that builds up the road

falling and rising,
rising and falling,
major catastrophe it creates.

But not, it bothers the identity of the supernova that
initiates,
nevertheless, you go on,
crossing, falling, burning, but the road remains,

Remains,
to provide you an offering, an opportunity,

just to define you and also to refine you.

and that's what you do,
with the four walls you see,
the more in a square less than to be.

21. Neck tie

Its triangular in shape
and if not in the neck can bring some to shame.

But, I disagree
to agree.

Neck tie is described as a noose
but it is actually a thing that makes one look mentally
loose

for reasons
that looks like treason

for not trying to work like ants
and receiving the money to wear torn pants

but repeatedly trying to achieve an outcome
for someone else's income

to keep the family in awe of aspiration
filled with stories of inspiration

but the tie is a liberation

from all aberration

of poverty
and instead to gain property.

It is the lenses
and the senses

that makes up the case
for the line of race

that people are up to complete
in order to compete

with the triangular shape cloth
that decides someone's worth.

22. A Stranger but mine

I saw a woman at a world I don't know
hoping to bond like a farmer wanting to sow

She seems deprived and lost with black eyes
dark and a fake smile beneath a sad eye as duplicate as a
dye

and it only shines bright on me like an orange
and makes me wonder about the cadence

that is landed to her by virtue of god's wonderful hands
made with atoms and emotions and grateful brands

In the palace where God resides and decides
how to form a being and make it sentient and proceeds
to describe

a stranger but mine in imagination
deprived of procrastination

and makes one to describe the stranger
with love in anger

and utter the words with grace
and quote the following and embrace

"When the wave of water ends
at the shore and the light of the sun,

falls on your cheek,
the nature smiles at your beauty,

with a little smirk
but with awe and a mist with joy."

and I fancied this visual
as I glanced at her being sensual

less sexual
more emotional

and a stranger in all scope who is fine
became all mine.